TEEN LIFE 411™

I HAVE AN STD.
NOW WHAT?

PHILIP WOLNY

ROSEN
PUBLISHING®

New York

Published in 2015 by The Rosen Publishing Group, Inc.
29 East 21st Street, New York, NY 10010

Copyright © 2015 by The Rosen Publishing Group, Inc.

First Edition

Library of Congress Cataloging-in-Publication Data

Wolny, Philip.
I have an STD. Now what?/Philip Wolny.—First edition.
    pages cm.—(Teen Life 411)
Includes bibliographical references and index.
ISBN 978-1-4777-7980-4 (library bound)
1. Sexually transmitted diseases—Juvenile literature. I. Title.
RC200.25.W65 2015
616.95'1—dc23
                                        2014008557

Manufactured in China

CONTENTS

A young man sits in the waiting room of a free clinic, waiting anxiously for news. He is called into a nurse's station and the door closes behind him. The nurse tells him he has tested positive for genital herpes. As the news sinks in, he barely hears the nurse run down a list of other places to visit for treatment.

Like millions of other young people in the United States, this young man was diagnosed with a sexually transmitted disease (STD). Adults and teens alike can catch STDs from having unprotected sex, and the rates of infection have risen dramatically in this country in the past two decades.

If you know little about STDs, finding out you have become infected with one can be pretty bad news. Going through your teenage years can be tough enough. Emotions run high as teens deal with school, family, and friends. New pressures also arise as an adolescent's body changes. Many teens just want to feel normal and accepted. For some, this need to belong involves experimenting with sex or sexual activity.

Teens might start having sex with several partners. Or they might remain monogamous (with just one partner). Suddenly, everything takes a turn for the worse: they find out they have an STD.

Many teens are caught completely by surprise when they find out they have been infected. One reason is that they may know little or even nothing about STDs. It is often hard to separate rumors, myths, and

Getting an STD can be troubling and embarrassing. However, getting over fear and shame and seeking help from health professionals is ultimately the only wise decision.

misconceptions from the medical facts. Young people, especially those who have never experienced major health problems before, might think, "It couldn't happen to me."

The truth is that anyone can get STDs because they do not discriminate. Statistics might show that certain groups could be more prone to infection than others, such as those who are very sexually active and intravenous drug users. But it only takes one time, one stroke of bad luck, to become infected.

Another misconception is that catching an STD means the end of the world. Many teenagers never show symptoms even if they get infections such as chlamydia, gonorrhea, HPV, or herpes. Others only suffer mild and rare outbreaks. A good segment of young people infected in the United States do not even know they are carriers.

On the other hand, not knowing can have serious consequences. Untreated STDs can lead to greater health problems, even life-threatening ones. Finding out what STDs are, how they are treated, and thinking about the aspects of your life that are affected by getting one are all important steps to becoming educated on this important topic. Many young people have too little information on a subject that can impact their health in dramatic ways. Certain symptoms and warning signs from your body will tell you that you may have an STD. Now what?

CHAPTER 1

What are STDs, really? How does someone know he or she has contracted, or caught, one? STDs include a wide variety of infections that are known to spread through sexual contact. Certain kinds can also be spread through other high-risk behaviors, such as intravenous (IV) drug use, and, very rarely, through blood transfusions during medical procedures.

Also known as venereal diseases (VD), they have been referred to more recently as sexually transmitted infections, or STIs. "STI" is sometimes used as a broader term, and includes infections from which someone may never suffer symptoms, even if he or she can potentially spread the infection to others. Some use the term "STD" when talking about a smaller pool of individuals: those who exhibit symptoms from "STIs." Still, the diseases themselves are commonly called STDs, and the term "STIs" can be used as well.

Different STDs have distinct causes. Some are caused by bacteria, such as chlamydia, syphilis, and gonorrhea (otherwise known as "the clap"). Others are viral infections, including herpes simplex virus 2, or genital herpes, and human papillomavirus, known as HPV. Another category of infection is caused by tiny organisms that do not fall into these

categories (neither bacteria nor viruses).

However, the one aspect they have in common is that most of them are far more easily spread through unprotected sex—that is, having sex without using a condom during vaginal, oral, or anal sex. Avoiding sexual activity completely, called abstinence, is the only way to avoid catching an STD. Using protection while having sex goes a long way toward preventing the spread of STDs but does not provide a surefire guarantee.

Having a partner you can trust and depend on goes a long way in terms of helping you deal with an STD infection.

Why It Happens: Risk Factors

There are many reasons that STD rates have increased among young people. For years, the United States has had the highest rates of infection in the industrialized world. One reason is misinformation. Many teenagers of both sexes have little real knowledge about what STDs are, or how they are spread.

A majority of teenagers do not have the slightest notion of how to safeguard their health, especially at an age when many are just starting to experiment with physical intimacy and having relationships in general. There are a number of risk factors that affect the chances of a person contracting STDs. Some of these are interrelated—that is, they depend on one another.

Youth and inexperience are also closely linked to the risk of catching STDs. Besides often being misinformed, teens might also be more susceptible to certain infections. Teen girls, for example, have a higher chance of infection in the cervix, a sensitive part of the reproductive system. If they do become infected with an STD, chances are they might not get diagnosed nor treated, and thus risk serious health consequences later. This possibility is especially true if they do not show symptoms until much later, when dealing with the resulting health issues is more difficult.

Sexual Partners and Promiscuity

The more partners someone has had, and the more sexual encounters, the greater chance the person has of catching something, no matter what his or her gender or sexual orientation.

Some teens become sexually promiscuous because of emotional issues. They seek escape or fulfillment because they suffer from depression or other ailments, such as attention deficit-hyperactive disorder (ADHD), or simply feel isolated or neglected by their peers or family. Some might feel pressured by a partner or their social group to have sex. If they become part of a group or clique whose members have casual sex, especially with multiple partners, there is a greater chance they will, too.

Unsurprisingly, teens who have multiple partners tend to pair up with others who have several partners. A common warning goes as follows: when you have sex with someone, you are really having sex with every person that person has had sex with before. Unless someone is completely honest, his or her partners have little idea of what they are getting into when they pick someone.

Other young people practice what is called "serial monogamy." They only have one partner at a time, but switch partners often. Although they are in an exclusive relationship, this might promote a false sense of

security. Tests for some STDs might not reveal an infection for some time, so that even partners who do the right thing and get tested might put each other at risk.

It is perfectly natural to want to try out new things and have new experiences. Sadly, anyone can contract an STD. Whether someone has five, ten, or more partners a year, or just one his or her entire high school career, he or she can contract something. However, being monogamous reduces the odds. Abstinence pretty much reduces those odds to zero.

Anyone who is planning to have sex should schedule routine gynecological and male genital

The company that teens keep is often a big influence on their behavior. Teens may trend toward promiscuity or monogamy depending on their social group or clique.

exams with her or his medical professional. These regular examinations enable doctors to ensure that their patients know how to protect themselves against getting STDs and help the medical professionals to determine whether someone has contracted an STD so that he or she can be treated for it as soon as possible.

Types of Sexual Activity and Risk

Although vaginal sex is the riskiest, many teens do not realize that oral and anal sexual activity expose them to comparable risks. American teens often engage in oral sex first. University of California pediatrics professor Bonnie Halpern-Felsher, who has conducted surveys on teens' sexual habits, told WebMD that teens "don't consider it a big deal" and that most of them did not consider having oral sex as risky.

Many young people are similarly misinformed or have a casual attitude toward anal sex. Even with the use of condoms, anal sex can be dangerous. Unprotected, it can be as just as risky as vaginal sex. This area of the body does not self-lubricate, and its fragile nature makes it more likely the skin inside will tear. This makes it easier for STDs to enter the victim's bloodstream, whether it is through the anus or penis. The anus is also

This diagram shows some of the main parts of the male and female human reproductive systems. STDs can infect and impair these vital organ systems.

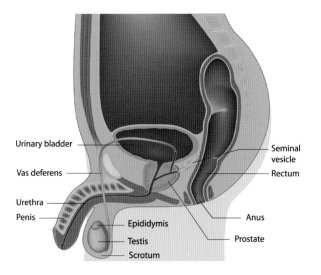

Urinary bladder

Vas deferens

Urethra

Penis

Epididymis

Testis

Scrotum

Seminal vesicle

Rectum

Anus

Prostate

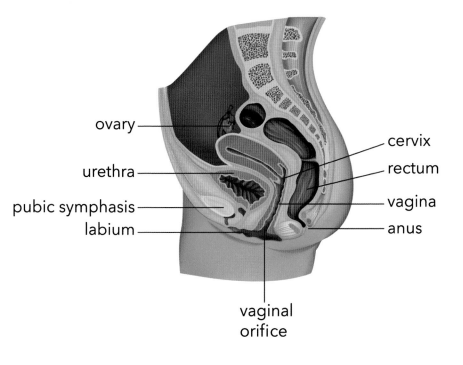

ovary

urethra

pubic symphasis

labium

cervix

rectum

vagina

anus

vaginal orifice

a welcoming place for bacteria because it is a warm and wet environment.

STDS are not only transmitted through exchanging semen, blood, or other bodily fluids during sex, but also through direct contact with a partner's infected body areas. Any type of sexual activity with a partner carries some risk. Certain STDs can spread between partners who use a condom, too. Sores and warts around the outside of the vagina or anus can be dangerous. Condoms and other barrier methods of contraception may not

Condoms: The Right Way and the Wrong Way

Wearing male and female condoms properly protects both you and your partner. If only one partner wears a condom, the condom loses much of its effectiveness at preventing STDs and pregnancy. This is true of both types of condoms, male or female. Users should learn how to put on or insert the condom correctly. Proper lubrication also prevents breakage and irritation of areas that can then also suffer tears and help expose the bloodstreams of one or both partners to STDs. In addition, it is recommended that male users wear condoms made only from latex, and only with water-based lubricants, because oil can degrade latex.

cover all the areas where STDs are lurking. Other birth control methods, such as spermicides and diaphragms, can reduce the risk of becoming pregnant, but they do not keep a person from getting STDs.

DRUGS, ALCOHOL, AND SEX: A DANGEROUS MIX

Some teens seek an escape from their problems through drug or alcohol use. Others might be emotionally healthy, but may make poor decisions and abuse drugs or alcohol, sometimes with dangerous consequences. Drugs and alcohol impair decision-making and lower a person's inhibitions. According to a 2012 survey of more than a thousand twelve- to seventeen-year-olds, conducted by the National Center on Addiction and Substance Abuse at Columbia University, about nine out of ten students in high school stated that their classmates were taking drugs, drinking alcohol, and smoking during the school day. Younger and inexperienced consumers of alcohol and drugs are more likely to abuse these substances.

Although people might avoid sex while they are sober, a few beers or pills make it more likely that they will engage in dangerous, casual encounters. They are also less likely to take precautions to prevent STDs. Young people who are under the influence of alcohol might not consider the risks of having sex with a stranger or casual acquaintance. They will be more likely to forget about protection or be pressured into sex without it.

Teens might also put themselves into dangerous positions. Blacking out while they are drinking puts users at risk for rape and other forms of sexual assault. In some cases, someone might not even be aware that he or she engaged in risky behavior at all. When they begin to experience STD symptoms, it is that much more difficult to track down who infected them.

It is advisable to avoid intoxication to lessen the chances of catching an STD. Also, teens can reduce their chances of catching STDs by avoiding sexual partners known to abuse drugs and alcohol.

Few measures eliminate all risks of STDs. Using condoms, like the ones pictured here in a drugstore display, is one of the most effective methods of preventing STD transmission.

NO ONE IS IMMUNE

Even emotionally healthy teens, and those in a monogamous relationship, in which two partners agree to be only with each other and no one else, can get an STD. However honest or kind a partner seems, his or her

A couple that decides to undergo STD screening—whether they go separately or together—shows that they are taking positive steps to protect their health.

sexual history might be very different from what he or she says. Many STD infections are preventable if two partners agree to get tested before engaging in sexual activity. Unfortunately, many teens avoid screening or simply do not think about it.

AVOIDING PANIC

Imagine waking up one day, going to the bathroom, and feeling a burning sensation when you urinate, or seeing some strange substance, or discharge, down there. For girls, the first sign of something amiss might be abdominal pain during sex or physical activity. Boys and girls might discover uncomfortable rashes or painful blisters in their genital regions. That moment can be tough for anybody. As hard as it seems, they should take a deep breath and try to remain calm.

A natural and common reaction might be to panic. Getting sick is bad enough, but it can be especially uncomfortable and scary when it happens in those regions of the body. It is important to stay calm and remember that millions of other teens are going through, or have gone through, a similar ordeal.

One of the largest studies, and first of its kind covering teenagers (by the Centers for Disease Control and Prevention [CDC] in 2008) determined that one in four teenage girls carries an STD, according to *USA Today.* More than 40 percent of those surveyed said they had sex and had an STD at one time or another. According to the U.S. Department of Health and Human Services, about 9.5 million teens and young adults (ages fifteen to twenty-four) every year are diagnosed with an STD.

Despite these troubling statistics, many teens do not consider themselves part of a high-risk group for infection. This misconception means that they do not even think of getting tested until symptoms arise. Even then, some simply ignore an outbreak and hope it goes away on its own.

EVERYTHING'S CHANGED...OR HAS IT?

Besides the initial shock, it is natural to overreact and believe that catching an STD is "the end of the world." Most teens who have had the misfortune of contracting one live normal, productive lives, especially if they tackle their problem early on. Those experiencing trouble in their lives often learn that there is some truth to the old saying, "Whatever doesn't kill you only makes you stronger."

Depending on the type of STD they contract, teens' lives may change in the smallest of ways, or require bigger adjustments. They might have to think about things that they did not have to worry about before—like taking precautions and having tough conversations with new boyfriends or girlfriends. They must be prepared to be straightforward and honest.

If you are infected, however, you should think about the things that led to your infection, and the steps you now need to take to protect your health and that of future partners. Teens also need to arm themselves with coping mechanisms for any other problems that can arise from getting the STD. These can include later health complications if the STD is left untreated, including infertility (the inability to have children) if it is a bacterial STD, and emotional issues such as depression. Some teens might already be predisposed to some of these conditions and might need to work extra hard and seek more help than others.

It might seem like a disaster, but it can be a learning opportunity and a chance to show you are strong enough to make the right decisions to take charge of the problem. Above all, having respect for yourself, and for others in your life, and being honest and realistic will go a long way in helping you out of your predicament.

There is no reason to feel ashamed, or to panic, if you think you have an STD. Most STDs are treatable, and many do not present serious health threats early on. The first real step, however, is to find out for sure.

These days, many people, including both young people and adults, make the mistake of self-diagnosing using the Internet. Looking online can be valuable to find helpful information, and to start the process. But it can also lead to false information and incorrect diagnoses. Even a smart person might mistake a headache or tiredness for something far more serious—a common rash, fungus, or urinary tract infection (UTI)—for an STD while searching the Internet in a panicked state.

A real STD diagnosis means visiting a doctor or other medical professional at a hospital or clinic to get tested. It's a good idea to get STD screening not just for the one infection you might be worried about, but also for the others for which you are at risk if you are sexually active. Sexually active people might have more than one STD.

MYTH

People with STDs become infected with them because they are sexually promiscuous.

FACT

Anyone can catch an STD, even someone having sex for the first time. People of all kinds, and from all walks of life, can catch one. STDs do not discriminate.

MYTH

STDs are spread through casual contact, and having people around with STDS is dangerous for uninfected people.

FACT

STDs are largely spread through unprotected sexual activity. It is highly unlikely to get an STD from nonsexual contact.

MYTH

You can easily tell if someone has an STD, especially if you see him or her naked.

FACT

Many people with STDs do not show symptoms, and even with those who do, one can never be certain if a particular symptom indicates an STD. Only proper medical screening and testing can diagnose STDs. Teens with STDs look like everybody else.

MYTHS AND FACTS

CHAPTER 2

WHAT DO YOU HAVE?

Making an appointment for an STD can be emotionally difficult. Some young people, and even many adults, have a fear of doctor's offices, hospitals, and clinics. They tell themselves they would rather not find out than get potentially bad or even terrible news. Remember: whatever happens, you will always be better off knowing than not knowing. Finding out early enough can even mean curing an STD painlessly. It can prevent health problems later and even save your life.

Many people are afraid of the testing itself, fearing it might be physically (or even emotionally) uncomfortable or painful. Ultimately, there's really nothing to it, and little beyond what someone might experience during a routine doctor's visit. Doctors or health workers will first ask about symptoms. If someone has physical symptoms, he or she will usually undergo a physical examination.

The doctor might take blood samples using a needle or a finger stick, and ask for a urine sample. Both are either tested on-site or sent away for analysis. STDs are also tested using swabs. A swab is a ball of cotton on the end of a long stick. The swab is used to take a sample of mucus, discharge, or other

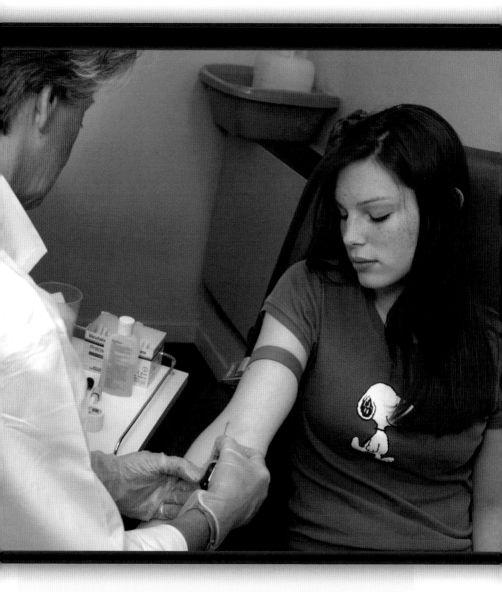

Blood tests are among the most common ways of screening for STDs and are far less painful and uncomfortable than many people fear them to be.

cells in areas that are likely affected, including the penis, vagina, throat, and the anal cavity. For some types of STDs, two or more methods are used to make a positive diagnosis.

WHERE TO GET TESTED?

Most people infected with STDs want to keep this fact secret, or at least restricted to the smallest number of people possible. Some might reveal their infection only to a doctor, while others will tell only a parent or family member. Anyone who has caught something has some important choices to make, and everyone has different needs and concerns. An immediate question is where and by whom to get tested.

Teens' first option for testing might be their family doctor. Teens concerned about their privacy can look up their state's rules on confidentiality. However, most states protect teens' privacy. If someone is at least the age of thirteen, a doctor or other health professional must respect the patient's wishes if he or she wishes to keep the nature of the visit, or any test results, confidential. The only exception is when the doctor fears for the teen's life, or for the lives of others.

However, teens might still need to investigate whether their parents might find out about their predicament in other ways. Depending on the area, and on the insurance rules, insurance companies might be required to mail a notice of what services were covered during a teen's medical visit.

For teens worried about affordability or insurance coverage, states (through a department of health) and communities may run free clinics that offer free STD screening. City or county health clinics might offer free testing certain days of the week, for example, as do hospital-associated ones.

Nonprofit organizations also offer free or inexpensive screening. Planned Parenthood is a well-known, nationwide organization that provides affordable screening. Charitable organizations might do so, too, and even some faith-based groups. Lesbian, gay, bisexual, and transgender (LGBT) community centers often offer testing services for their target communities, but accept walk-in patients of any kind. Many organizations offer sliding-scale payment. Patients pay only what they can afford. Some locations might also offer on-site treatment, or assist in securing psychological counseling to help teens through the initial tough times following an STD diagnosis.

LOW-COST AND FREE SCREENINGS

FINDING THE CULPRIT

The different types of infections generally fall into categories depending on what causes them. Like other diseases, such as the flu, common cold, and other everyday ailments, most STDs are caused by microorganisms, living things that are too tiny to see without a microscope or other instruments. These include bacteria, viruses, and other organisms.

BACTERIAL STDs

Bacteria are very tiny organisms that inhabit the world. Many are completely harmless. They exist everywhere, invisible to the naked eye. Certain bacteria cause STDs, however, and these are generally considered among the least serious because bacterial STDs can usually be cured. Bacterial STDs account for some of the most widespread health crises for young people today.

Chlamydia

The bacterium *Chlamydia trachomatis* is responsible for the STD known as chlamydia. It is the most common bacterial STD nationwide, infecting about three million annually, according to the

This digital art shows a microscopic view of the bacterium *Chlamydia trachomatis*. The bacterium is magnified thousands of times larger than its actual size.

CDC. It is widespread, but three out of four women who are infected with it never suffer any symptoms. The same goes for about 50 percent of males. Many never seek treatment.

Still, those experiencing symptoms get them within five to ten days of infection. For women, these can be quite uncomfortable, such as abdominal pain, a painful or burning sensation during urination and sexual activity, vaginal or anal swelling, and vaginal discharge. Women may also bleed after having sex, or randomly bleed even between menstrual periods, and suffer fevers.

Men also experience painful or burning urination, penile discharge, and swelling and pain in the testicles and around the anus. Both men and women might experience anal itching and bleeding. Other parts of the body can be affected by chlamydia, too, including the eyes and throat.

Gonorrhea

A similar bacterial infection is gonorrhea. It is sometimes confused with chlamydia because of similar symptoms, but is about a third as widespread among sexually active people. Gonorrhea carriers often carry chlamydia as well. Caused by the bacterium *Neisseria gonorrhoeae*, gonorrhea affects the female's cervix and vagina, the male's penis, and the urethra, anus, and throat of both sexes. It has been nicknamed "the clap" or "the drip," due to the discharge it causes in both sexes.

Some symptoms of gonorrhea for women include abdominal pain, vaginal discharge, pain during urination and sex, fever, nausea, bleeding between periods, menstrual irregularities, and swelling and tenderness of the vulva. Men endure discharge from the penis and burning and pain during frequent urination. Their testicles may also become swollen. Anal itching, painful bowel movements, and itching and soreness of the throat may affect both sexes.

Four out of five women never show symptoms, while nine out of ten men do. If they appear, they usually manifest within two to ten days of infection. Early symptoms for both sexes are often mild and may be confused with other health conditions. Doctors may screen for this STD by testing discharge from the anus, urethra, or vagina, use a cotton swab for samples from various genital areas or the throat, or test the urine.

Syphilis

The *Treponema pallidum* bacterium causes one of the more serious STDs out there: syphilis. In earlier human history, syphilis was responsible for much death and suffering. If left untreated, it is still very dangerous, and an infected person can go through four stages of syphilis infection: primary, secondary, latent, and tertiary, or late-stage infection.

When people first catch it, they suffer an ulcer at the point of infection, sometimes called a chancre, which shows up any time from ten days to three months after exposure. This chancre may be painless and unseen, especially if it occurs inside the body, and is the primary stage.

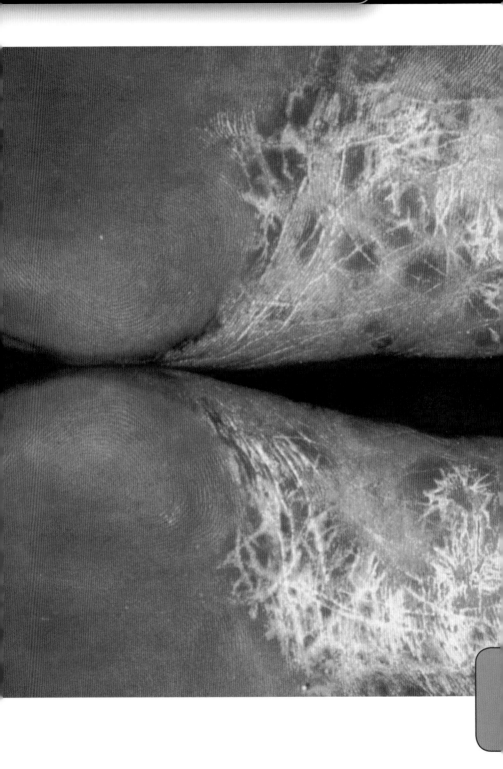

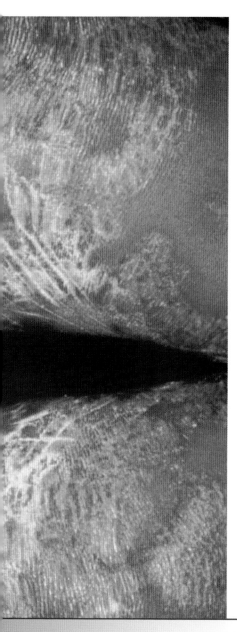

The secondary stage occurs within three to six weeks after the chancre forms. Small brown sores accompany a skin rash, which can afflict the whole body or particular areas, but almost always appear on a victim's soles of the feet and palms of the hands. The sores and rash are actively contagious. Other symptoms may include mild fever, fatigue, sore throat, hair loss, and swelling in the lymph glands. Secondary symptoms come and go, disappearing without treatment, over the course of one or two years.

VIRAL STDs

Unfortunately, the antibiotics that cure bacterial

Syphilis (*Treponema pallidum*) infection is shown here, manifesting itself as sores and skin loss on the soles of a person's feet.

STDs do not work against viruses. Viruses are not alive in the sense that bacteria are—they are infectious agents that can reproduce only in the cells of other living things. This aspect makes most viral infections incurable, including the many viruses that cause the common cold, and flu viruses. However, many of these are treatable, including viral STDs, and a few have even had effective vaccines developed to prevent them.

One of the most common viral STDs is human papillomavirus (HPV). There are more than one hundred types of HPV known to exist worldwide. Most are actually harmless. Thirty of these are spread via sexual contact, and, like many who get bacterial STDs, many infected people never show symptoms. The most common symptoms, when they do occur, are genital warts.

Genital warts—also known as venereal warts or *Condylomata acuminata*—arise in or around a person's genitals. They are soft and flesh-colored, sometimes appearing in clusters. They can be raised or flat. Women get them on the vulva, cervix, and near the vagina. They may appear on tip or shaft of a male's penis or on the scrotum, or near the anus.

Most genital warts are visible and easily identified by doctors. HPV tests may also include taking cervical samples from women, using vinegar to whiten invisible warts in the genital region. A Pap smear may also reveal that a woman has a cervical HPV infection.

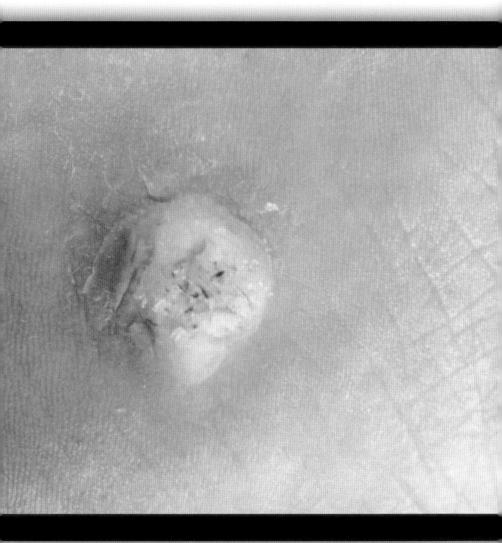

A genital wart—known also by its scientific name, *Condylomata acuminata*—is a common symptom of the human papillomavirus. This one is perineal, flaring up near the sufferer's rectum.

One of the other common viral STDs is herpes, also known as *Herpes genitalis*, is caused by one of two strains of the herpes virus, HSV-1 and HSV-2, though most sufferers of genital herpes have traditionally gotten it from exposure to HSV-2.

Herpes symptoms can appear within days of infection. Many sufferers mistake it for other conditions or diseases, or they do not show symptoms at all. Early symptoms can include: a burning feeling in the genitals or anus; leg pain or pain in the buttocks or genitals; vaginal discharge; and feelings of abdominal swelling or pressure.

Soon, red bumps appear where the herpes virus first entered the body. These become blisters, and then painful open sores. These lesions can appear on the mouth, penis, or vagina, depending on the type of activity that led to the infection. Women may have sores in their vagina or

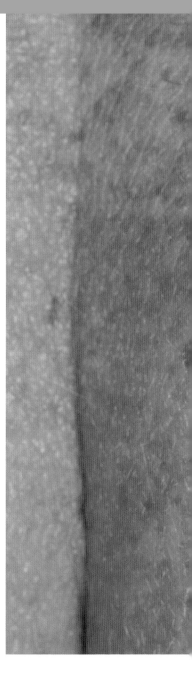

This close-up view shows a woman's blisters that were produced by the herpes simplex virus, a type of virus that causes herpes. Contact with such blisters is one method of the transmission and spread of the virus.

cervix, while both men and women get them in the urinary tract. These sores eventually heal, typically leaving no scars. The first outbreak can include glands swelling in the groin, vaginal discharge, painful or difficult urination, fever, headache, and aching muscles.

Hepatitis B

Less common but no less dangerous are the various forms of hepatitis. All strains of hepatitis can harm the liver and one's health in general, but the most common one that is spread through unprotected sex is the hepatitis B virus. About 90 percent of infected people experience acute hepatitis B. Flu-like symptoms, fatigue, dark urine and light-colored feces, along with jaundice—a yellowing of the skin—are common symptoms that may last a few months but then go away for life. These appear within a couple of months, and typically disappear by nine months, but might last longer.

About 10 percent become chronic carriers, infected for life. Hepatitis patients who do not know they are infected, or who avoid treatment, put themselves at risk for liver damage, called cirrhosis, or even liver cancer.

HIV/AIDS

Perhaps the most frightening STD is acquired immunodeficiency syndrome (AIDS), caused by the human immunodeficiency virus (HIV). HIV attacks the immune system of human beings. It kills the body's CD4 cells, also called T-helper cells, which assist the human body in fighting off diseases and infection. AIDS is the end stage of HIV infection, when much of the immune system has been harmed. AIDS patients can easily die from common infections that healthy people simply fight off, such as the flu.

HIV infection is more difficult to detect than other STDs. Many people do not exhibit symptoms, which varies greatly among patients. Warning signs might not appear until someone has full-blown AIDS. By that time, it is far more difficult to treat the effects of the disease. Warning signs include: rapid weight loss, a dry cough, extended bouts of diarrhea, fatigue, swelling in the lymph glands of the groin, neck, and armpit areas, fever and night sweats, colored blotches, white spots and strange blemishes on the skin or other parts of the body, pneumonia, and memory loss, depression, or unexplained mental disorders.

The most common tests for HIV/AIDS look for the presence of antibodies, blood proteins that are created when viruses or other foreign invaders enter the body. After someone is infected, it takes at least three months for the antibodies to appear. Other newer screening techniques test for HIV's genetic material. Most tests use blood samples or samples of oral fluid, which are collected by swabbing the inside of someone's mouth, as well as urine tests.

Depending on the test, results can be available within a couple of days and can take as long as two weeks. In recent years, rapid testing has been developed that produces results within twenty minutes. A positive result is usually backed up by a different type of HIV test, just in case the earlier test returns a false positive.

Besides sharing intravenous needles, the most common way HIV/AIDS is transmitted is through unprotected sex. Victims have been infected by giving or receiving oral sex, but this is more rare.

OTHER STDS

A few other STDs are caused by larger parasitic organisms, creatures that depend on other living things to survive without providing any benefit. One example is pubic lice, commonly known as "crabs," which are also transmitted between sexual partners. A condition called scabies, caused by an insect-like creature called a scabies mite, can be transmitted through sexual contact. Crabs and

This view of a scabies mite (*Sarcoptes scabiei*) has been magnified hundreds of times. These mites, ranging in size from about .004 to .01 inch (0.1 to 0.3 millimeter), are transmitted both through having sex and by casual contact.

scabies often cause intense itching, and crabs can also cause someone to feel run-down, or have a mild fever. Both organisms are easily treated with creams that can be applied to the affected areas. For scabies, prescription medication needs to be applied all over the body, whereas treatment for crabs is available over the counter, without a prescription.

Another common STD is trichomoniasis, or "trich," caused by tiny creatures called protozoa. Women infected with trich experience vaginal discharge, vaginal blood spotting, itching and swelling in the groin area, and the need to urinate often. Men rarely suffer symptoms, but experience discharge and frequent urination that causes pain and burning. Trich is easily cured with prescription medication.

1. What are the different ways that one can test for STDs?

2. How reliable are different types of STD tests? Does someone need to take more than one?

3. What are the possible side effects from antibiotics or antiviral medications and treatments?

4. Do other medical conditions make it more likely that I will suffer worse from my STD than others?

5. Can I discuss my STD and sexual activities in private, or do my parents have to be informed?

6. Can I receive affordable or free treatment for my STD?

7. Has the STD damaged my body in any way, or did I treat it in time?

8. Can I take a single-dose cure or do I need to take regular medication for my STD?

9. Should I get tested for all other possible STDs?

10. Will I have to deal with long-term health effects because of my STD?

10 GREAT QUESTIONS TO ASK YOUR DOCTOR

Finding out what exactly has affected your health, and how serious it is, is an important first step. Any teen should be proud of having the strength to face his or her fears in this way. Very few, however, should face such ordeals of treatment and recovery alone, even if they can do these unassisted.

One of the first ordeals might be the waiting game. Some STDs can be diagnosed immediately, right at a medical office. For others, the patient might have to wait a short while for the results. This wait can be stressful for anybody.

Dealing with STDs sooner rather than later is always best. This action may not be feasible if someone does not have a clue that he or she is even infected, especially those who never exhibit symptoms. For this reason, even low-risk teens should get tested regularly if they have had sexual contact of any kind. The earlier you know, the better chance to cure or prevent worse symptoms from developing later.

ANTIBIOTICS TO THE RESCUE

All three of the common bacterial STDs—chlamydia, gonorrhea, and syphilis—can be cured at the earliest stages. The most common and effective treatments for these STDs are antibiotics. These medicines are really poisons that are designed to kill disease-causing bacterial cells while leaving the cells of the human body unharmed.

Many patients suffer from chlamydia and gonorrhea at the same time, and doctors often prescribe combinations of certain antibiotics to treat both simultaneously, even if only one of the two has been diagnosed.

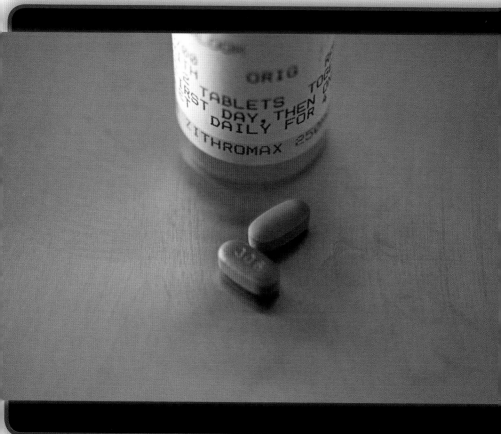

Zithromax, shown here, is a trade name for azithromycin, an antibiotic drug used to treat bacterial infections, including the STDs chlamydia and gonorrhea, as well as illnesses such as bronchitis.

When a first round of antibiotic treatment is completed, a doctor will perform another diagnostic test to ensure that the infection has been cured. Gonorrhea might take only twenty-four hours to cure, while chlamydia might take a week. The latter is either treated with a single antibiotic dose, or a course of treatment for about a week, though sometimes treatment lasts as long as two weeks. Patients being treated for either must abstain from sexual activity until treatment is done and all symptoms have disappeared. They must also take all the medication they are told to take. Missing doses of medication might make it less effective, or extend the amount of time someone has to take the drug.

Years ago, gonorrhea was easily treatable with a single antibiotic dose. Nowadays, strains, or types, of gonorrhea have become stronger, and many people need ever more powerful antibiotics, and often combinations of two or more antibiotics, to successfully beat back these bacteria. Over time, the standard treatments for STDs might change.

Doctors prescribe penicillin for syphilis infections. They substitute antibiotics for those with penicillin allergies. Certain patients might need higher doses to fight their infections. All in all, syphilis is one of the most easily treated STDs. Most patients require only a single injection of penicillin, which kills syphilis within about twenty-four hours. Those undergoing syphilis treatment must not have sex until their sores are completely healed. Active syphilis sores increase someone's chances of catching HIV/AIDS, too.

BACTERIAL STDs: THE BIG PICTURE

It is very important to diagnose and treat gonorrhea, chlamydia, and syphilis early on. The initial discomforts of chlamydia, for example, are nothing compared to what happens if this bacterial STD is left untreated, especially for females. The infection can move into a woman's upper reproductive tract and cause certain reproductive organs to swell and become scarred. This condition is known as pelvic inflammatory disease (PID).

Some patients of PID might benefit from antibiotics or anti-inflammatory (anti-swelling) treatments, but for many the only choice is surgery. Other possible effects of untreated PID include ectopic pregnancy, in which a fetus develops outside a woman's uterus. This condition almost always results in the pregnancy failing, and is life-threatening to the mother. Chlamydia is also a leading cause of infertility among women. Other problems might include pre-term birth, pneumonia, and infant eye infections. Chlamydia is a leading cause of preventable blindness in infants worldwide, too.

Males are not off the hook if they fail to treat chlamydia, either. They can also sometimes suffer from epididymitis. This condition is an infection of part of the testicles that cause them to shrink and work less effectively. Infertility is also a possible result.

Gonorrhea, similarly, must also be taken care of earlier rather than later, as it results in many of the same

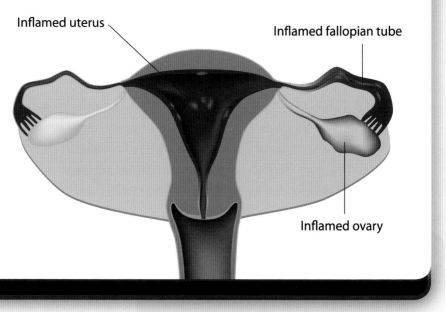

Pelvic Inflammatory Disease

Inflamed uterus

Inflamed fallopian tube

Inflamed ovary

Pelvic inflammatory disease (PID), which is shown in this illustration, can include symptoms such as inflammation of a woman's fallopian tubes, uterus, and ovaries.

long-term health problems as chlamydia: PID, ectopic pregnancy, and infertility. Pregnant sufferers can pass along the infection in the form of gonorrhea conjunctivitis, which, if left untreated, can also lead to infant blindness.

Not everyone will react to antibiotic treatments in the same way. You might feel no side effects, or only mild ones, or you could feel ill. Some side effects include nausea and vomiting, while women sometimes get yeast infections. Doctors prescribing these medicines should inquire about your potential allergies, and what other medications you might be taking. For example, erythromycin mixes badly with some common medications, raising the chances of a heart attack. Other antibiotics, such as levofloxacin, can cause damage to the tendons—they can swell the elbows, shoulders, and hands soon after treatment starts. Teens under eighteen years old, and pregnant patients, should avoid ciprofloxacin or ofloxacin because these can possibly damage their muscles and skeletal structure in the future.

Antibiotics: Side Effects

For men, untreated gonorrhea infection presents similar risks to those arising from chlamydia. These signs include pain, swelling, and damage to the testicular area resulting in scar tissue and eventual infertility. Arthritis, skin irritations and problems, and a host of other infections in the organs have also been linked to lingering gonorrhea infections.

During its later stages, no medicine will remedy the organs and body tissues damaged by syphilis. For about two-thirds of infected people, syphilis enters a latent

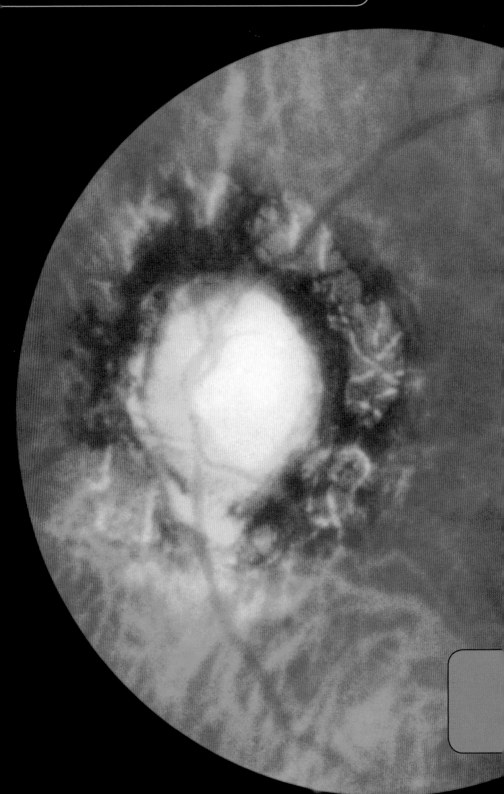

stage, with no symptoms, during which time the person is no longer contagious. However, the unlucky one-third who develop late, or tertiary, syphilis enter a particularly dangerous stage of the disease. The bacteria flare up and can severely damage many organ systems in the body, and can destroy the eyes, bones, joints, nervous system, heart, and nearly any other part of the body. Blindness, brain damage, heart disease, and even death are not uncommon for those suffering from this stage.

VIRAL STDs: IN THE LONG RUN

Viral STDs, unlike bacterial ones, are not curable. This fact does not mean one will suffer permanently, however. Medicine has become more advanced in recent years, offering those infected even better chances at living normal lives.

With genital herpes, some sufferers experience few ill effects.

This color-enhanced view of a human eye shows the retina of the subject infected with neuro-ocular syphilis. Untreated, this STD has been known to cause blindness.

Outbreaks can occur as often as a few times a year for some, while others have only one or two the rest of their lives. For the former, these flare-ups can actually decrease in severity and duration over time.

Still, outbreaks can include unseen or unde-tected sores, which make it even more likely that a person might unknowingly spread the virus.

There is no cure yet for herpes. Sufferers can take antiviral medications, especially when they feel an outbreak coming on. These drugs work by stopping the herpes virus from multiplying itself in the body. Antivirals can help treat existing outbreaks, or limit the time that outbreaks stick around. Aciclovir is an antiviral drug used to treat herpes. Swallowing tablets or taking the drug intravenously is recommended for more serious cases. Aciclovir is also available as a topical cream to apply to sores. Another antiviral is famciclovir, which is in tablet form and taken orally.

Be ready, however, for possible side effects when taking antivirals. These might include headaches, nausea and vomiting, rashes, tremors, and, for a very small minority, a possibility of seizures. Most patients endure no side effects, or extremely mild ones, from these medications.

Some doctors will prescribe suppressive therapy if a patient suffers many outbreaks each year. This approach involves taking daily antivirals to prevent

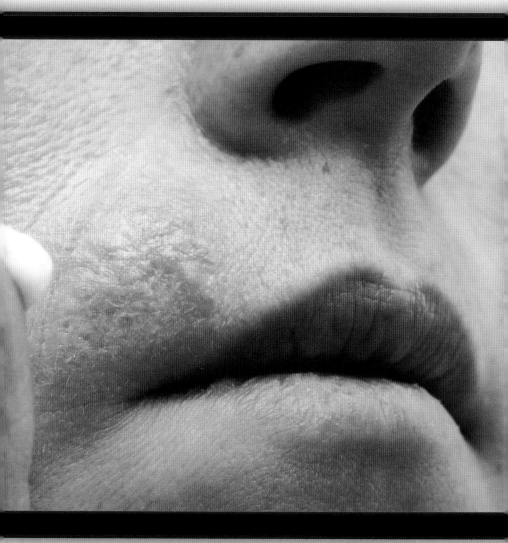

A patient applies an antiviral cream to a herpes cold sore. Such creams are among the most frequently sought prescription medications for this common viral infection.

outbreaks. Any antiviral medications can have potential side effects, and these may vary greatly among different people. As with antibiotics, only doctors can prescribe antivirals, and every patient seeking treatment should ask about possible side effects. Doctors will also determine if their patients possess any possible allergies to any ingredients of these antiviral treatments, especially life-threatening ones.

There are also other options for teens hoping to relieve milder herpes outbreaks. These include self-care at home and over-the-counter pain relievers to deal with any pain from sores. Using warm water and soap to gently cleanse areas where sores occur may help relieve pain, and properly drying after bathing is recommended. Avoid using bandages on sores because exposure to the air quickens healing. One should also avoid wearing nylon or synthetic underwear. Girls should avoid pantyhose or tights made from those materials. Your best bet is to keep the affected regions, especially the genital area, dry, and to wear loose-fitting cotton clothing.

HPV: To Treat or Not to Treat?

As with herpes, there are no known cures for HPV. In some cases, if there are no symptoms, many doctors will opt not to directly treat HPV because many carriers eventually defeat HPV with their own immune systems. Treatment of HPV means dealing with the genital warts themselves. These come and go for most sufferers, while for others they may stick around and grow. Various creams and solutions are prescribed to treat warts.

For women, the major concern surrounding HPV is its link to cervical cancer. Certain strains of the virus indeed turn cells cancerous, and not only in the woman's cervix. Other parts of the body for both sexes can potentially become cancerous with the presence of the high-risk HPV types. The body will usually clear the infection on its own, but anyone diagnosed with HPV should undergo screening periodically to guard for this problem.

If cells become abnormal from HPV, they can be removed by freezing them, a process called cryotherapy. Others require more serious surgery. Conization, or a cone biopsy, removes the HPV-affected cells. A process called loop electrosurgical excision procedure (LEEP) uses electric currents to remove them. The problem is that wart removal does nothing to cure the underlying HPV virus. No one can predict when warts or abnormal cells might grow back.

If you suffer from HPV, you may be so embarrassed by the occasional outbreaks that you will opt for such treatments. They might not be ideal for everyone, and many go away on their own. Getting treatment might mean using a parent or guardian's insurance, or having someone else pay for it. You must weigh whether you want to get rid of genital warts so badly that you do not mind enduring the procedures. Ask doctors about the

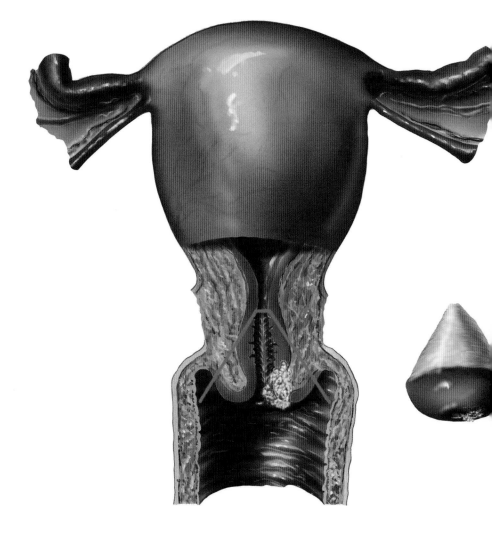

success rates and procedures themselves before making any hasty decisions.

Although it is too late for those infected with HPV, hope remains for those who are not yet sexually active. Recently developed HPV vaccines can protect against many forms of the viral infection, especially for those that may lead to cervical cancer. They are recommended for boys and girls from the ages of eleven and twelve. The HPV vaccines are given as a series of three shots over a period of six months to protect against infection.

HIV TREATMENT

Like other viral infections, HIV has no cure. It can be ten years or more after infection before warning signs appear, though a few people get them much sooner. When first identified as a disease in the early 1980s, catching HIV was considered a death sentence. Treatment of this life-threatening STD has come a long way since then. Many infected with HIV can live long, productive lives.

Still, there is no right course of treatment for any one patient because results can vary. There are also many different routes one can take to limit HIV's damage to the immune system. Doctors have devised something called combination therapy, in which several different drugs, called antiretrovirals, are used as a cocktail to treat HIV

This artwork shows the upper vagina *(lower center)* of the female reproductive system. At right, a cone-shaped section of tissue has been removed using cervical conization, a therapy that removes precancerous cells.

infection, otherwise known as highly active antiretroviral therapy (HAART). These drugs help control the amount of HIV in your body. Patients also keep track of their CD4 cells, or white blood cells, to determine how healthy they still are, and whether the drugs are working.

Many people are still split as to whether patients should begin treatments such as HAART before actually suffering physically from HIV's effects. They believe that the way the drugs help early on may actually make someone's chances worse later when his or her health actually declines. Depending on the person, HAART and other therapies are also known to cause nausea, vomiting, diarrhea, aches, fever, numbness, fatigue, dizziness, chills, insomnia, headaches, and a host of other uncomfortable side effects. Different combinations of therapy can also be extremely expensive.

Teens infected with HIV might not suffer the truly negative effects of infection, including AIDS, until years later, when they are already well into adulthood. For them, it might seem like a waiting game to get sick, but there are plenty of things one can do to maintain a healthy immune system that involve diet, exercise, stress reduction, and a positive outlook. Regular, frequent screenings to check on one's health are also very important.

An example of highly active antiretroviral therapy (HAART) is seen here, with Tenofovir (blue), Raltegravir (reddish), and Lamivudine (gray) pills.

CHAPTER 4

DEALING WITH STDS

It is recommended that someone diagnosed with an STD tell a parent, guardian, or other trusted relative, or even simply a supportive friend, teacher, or school counselor. Getting past the initial shame might be hard, but it is much easier than it seems. It is also well worthwhile for the potential support that the person can give you. Isolation usually makes things worse. Without another person to confide in, problems always seem bigger and harder to manage.

You can seek counseling from a medical professional, too. Many clinics that offer screening have specialists whose main job is helping teens out during such a difficult time. They are trained to be accepting and nonjudgmental.

You might not be ready to confide in somebody just yet. If not, consider calling a hotline to talk to a specialist trained to help teens who have STDs. Talking to someone anonymously, where both your identity and the counselor's are unknown, might be a good way to become comfortable with sharing your anxiety, while building up strength to confide in someone else. For example, organizations such as the AIDS Action Committee (AAC), Planned Parenthood, and the CDC, among many others, provide local and national phone

Medical professionals, especially those who are trained to work with teens, are uniquely equipped to answer questions and concerns about STDs.

hotlines and Internet resources for teens with STDs who need help.

A religious teen might also turn to a member of the local clergy. Whatever religion, faith, or house of worship one turns to, there might be a member of that community who also specializes in helping young people through such crises.

Another option for receiving emotional support is to visit a support group. Doctors, health professionals, social workers, therapists, and psychologists usually can provide referrals to support groups. Being around others who are in the same boat can be an incredibly powerful way to overcome the fear, shame, and embarrassment that people who are infected often feel.

These days, one can even turn to help online. If a teen is too shy, or even too far away to travel to a physical one, an online support group can be especially empowering to help with long-term coping and recovery issues. Doctors and other health professionals can help find a reputable, trustworthy site. You may find the answers to questions you were curious about and even make friends with other people posting to an online message board. Others may help out with links to blogs and other sites where people tell their stories. Doing an Internet search for herpes or other STDs, for example, will yield various Tumblrs and other online communities dedicated to letting those who have been infected get help, complain, and get useful information. If you need to reach out, seek out well-known groups and organizations with proven track records. Check with your medical professional for referrals to secure online support groups. Your state health department website will probably list trustworthy links. But remember that not everyone online has your best intentions in mind. Do not reveal personal information that can identify you to strangers. In addition, be mindful of discussing your infection on social media, blogs, or other sites. You never know who might discover your identity and use this information to hurt you.

Ultimately, though, you have the power. No one can force you to tell someone else about your challenges if you don't want to, or if you are afraid. It is important to know that you have options and you need not deal with an STD alone.

THE BLAME GAME

A natural reaction is to blame yourself, or your partner, for getting an STD infection. But only the worst type of person would intentionally spread an STD to someone else. Plenty of teens spread STDs without even knowing they are infected. Even those who know they have an STD and don't tell a partner aren't necessarily bad people. They might be misinformed, or wishing so badly they didn't have one that they ignore the problem. In the end, playing the "blame game" is a losing battle. Trying to figure out who to blame just distracts from the real task at hand: getting help for the disease.

COPING WITH STDS

Dealing emotionally with a new STD diagnosis is challenging. The immediate months following this discovery might be particularly tough. This period is the time to arm yourself with some coping mechanisms. Many of these are questions you should ask yourself when you have doubts or are feeling really down about your situation.

Depending on the STD, everyone's experience in coping is different. A young woman with herpes, for instance, who gets only a few mild outbreaks through her teen years, will endure less stress than one who gets sores a few times a year. They both, however, might experience shame and feel sorry for themselves at some point. "Will anyone want to date or ever fall in love with me?" "How do I tell a new partner? Will they stop liking me?" "Will I pass on this disease to my child if I ever have children?" These are common concerns and questions.

If you have an STD, you must realize that, although it might change your life, it does not end it, especially if you look after your health. A mild case of something might just be occasionally inconvenient. How much will your life change, really? Will it prevent you from finding happiness, finding a partner, doing well in school, or pursuing hobbies, sports, and other things you enjoy? For the vast majority of STD carriers and/or sufferers, the answer will be *no*.

Think of a herpes outbreak as simply bad luck, much like you would a cold or the flu. In fact, most of the time, STDs will not even take you out of commission like other common illnesses do. With some rare exceptions, you can still go to school, play sports, and take part in other

STD sufferers can boost their immune systems and hence help prevent flare-ups by embracing physical fitness, including competitive sports.

activities, see your friends, and pretty much do everything else you enjoyed before the STD came into your life.

Negative Coping Strategies: How Not to Act

A natural fear for any infected person is the fear that potential partners will not want to date you. A negative way of coping with this fear is by doing nothing, and by hiding your status from a boyfriend or girlfriend. This kind of behavior is especially negative if you realize you are currently having an outbreak, when certain STDs are even more contagious.

It is an irresponsible and selfish decision, ultimately. The only thing it accomplishes is putting another person at risk. This decision also assumes that no one will want to be close to you if you reveal the truth. In reality, you never know how others will react. Imagine how they will react, however, if they find out you knowingly infected them with HPV, herpes, or gonorrhea.

Another negative coping strategy is attempting to escape your problems through the abuse of alcohol or illegal or prescription drugs. Ironically, many teens who catch STDs because they made bad decisions while intoxicated also fall back on being drunk or high to escape the shame and depression that catching an STD might cause. Not only does substance abuse make matters worse, it can even jeopardize your health and make STD outbreaks more likely.

Other negative behaviors might encompass self-destructive conduct that rises out of anger and low self-esteem. This behavior might include self-harm, or even engaging in sex with many partners while knowing one is infected. For some, the pain and shame of an STD can make them try to do anything to distract themselves from the facts, even at the risk of doing things that will eventually break down their self-esteem and confidence. It is exactly those qualities that infected people need, however, as they move on with their lives.

PARTNERS: PAST AND PRESENT

When you find out you have an STD, you must also take the difficult step of letting others know. It might be embarrassing or awkward to contact someone, especially if it is after a bad breakup or other painful circumstance. In some cases, it might be difficult to retrace your steps to figure out when you contracted something, or from whom. For others, it might be relatively simple.

However, making an honest and active attempt to contact a former partner and warn him or her that that person might also have an STD is the right thing to do. Be prepared for a former partner who might not take this information so well, and might react angrily or attempt to cut you down in other ways. This reaction might happen even if you know for certain that the individual was the one who passed the STD to you.

Another major life change arising from STD infection is adjusting your sexual and dating habits. This adjustment includes the difficult talk one must have with new partners. Dealing with past partners openly and honestly about an STD can arm a teen for this next stage, too. Many teens with STDs might avoid intimacy with others, or avoid getting close to someone, even if sex is not involved in the relationship.

Having the talk is necessary whether the partner is a serious one or a more casual one. It is perhaps easier when someone is dating an individual seriously because he or she has established

Many young people fear "the Big Talk," the moment when they reveal their STD to a partner. However, such honesty is not only liberating but also the ethical and moral thing to do.

more trust and intimacy in the relationship. The fear of rejection as a young person dating is bad enough without the hidden shame of having an STD. Someone who just met you might not want to take this chance, and you must be prepared for rejection. Some counselors recommend preparing a script and practicing it in a mirror, or role-playing the situation with a trusted friend or family member. They also advise being confident and calm when telling someone, thus not worrying them that the news is worse than it really is.

Many teens might be surprised at how understanding others will be. With STD rates as high as they have been, chances are a potential partner might already have dated another person with one. They might even reveal one of their own. Also, a partner who is willing to take precautions and work around your condition is worth more than one who will retreat or abandon you. Whatever happens, it is important to realize that you are not alone, and that you deserve respect and love as much as anyone else. Having a normal dating life and a relationship are possible.

It is important to remember that although telling a partner is what you should do, no one can tell you when to inform him or her. Just as few people tell their whole life story early in a relationship, no one should feel they have to reveal an HPV infection on the first date. It is only if he or she will do anything that puts the other person at any risk of infection—namely, any kind of sexual activity, protected or not—that the individual should feel an obligation to do the right thing.

TELLING YOUR PARENTS

For many teens, telling their parents that they have an STD is tough. It is often harder than telling a current or former partner about it. They fear the parents' anger and disappointment, judgment or punishment, or even simple embarrassment.

Teens are often embarrassed to talk with their parents about sensitive topics, even if there is nothing wrong, and even if they have an otherwise healthy relationship. A study commissioned by Planned Parenthood, *Family Circle* magazine, and New York University's Center for Latino Adolescent and Family Health (CLAFH) in 2012 reported that half of all

Telling parents about an STD infection is one of the toughest things anybody ever has to do. Embarrassment and anxiety often keep STD sufferers from seeking their parents' help.

teens felt uncomfortable discussing sex with their parents.

A mother or father might have no idea that their teen has become sexually active, and having the subject come up for the first time because of an STD can be extremely awkward. Some teens might also fear punishment or tension with parents who are strict, conservative, or particularly religious. There might be tension between you and your parents merely because of the normal growing pains of adolescence.

If telling your parents is not a recourse, or might even lead to harm or other negative consequences, you must consider your options carefully. An aunt, uncle, or grandparent might be more sympathetic and helpful. As an adult who is close to you, the person might even help to work things out with your immediate family if your STD diagnosis causes a stir. Who else you can turn to depends on your situation. It might be a sibling, cousin, friend, or a mental health professional. Whomever it is, if you are infected and feeling like you are drowning in your problems, telling someone can really be a comfort.

ON YOUR SIDE

On the other hand, if someone's parents are approachable, they can be a tremendous help for a teen who has contracted an STD. They can provide much-needed moral support. In addition, they can help someone younger and inexperienced seek treatment, counseling, and other assistance.

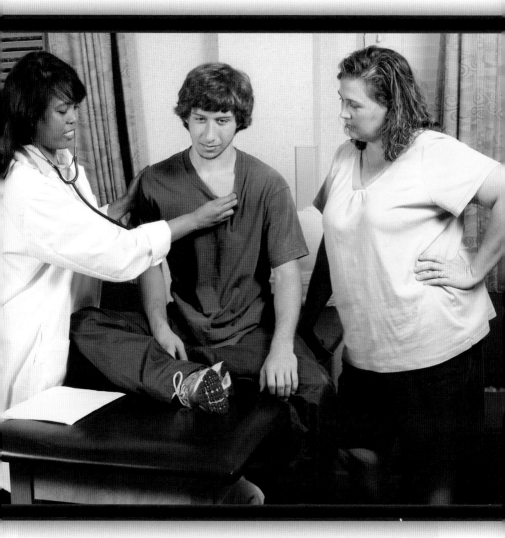

With some kind of support, such as from family or friends, STD sufferers are more likely to seek the diagnosis and treatment they require.

Weighing your options can enable you to see things a bit more clearly. On one hand, for instance, there is that potentially awkward and perhaps painful conversation about catching an STD. Many teens choose to avoid it. On the other hand, there is the potential feeling of relief of revealing a painful secret, and knowing that your parents will be on your side while you are on the road to recovery.

It is also more likely that parents will be able to give you assistance with money for medicine and medical visits, and other resources, such as a ride to a faraway clinic. Even if you earn your own money from a job in your spare time, you might need the aid. It is one less thing to worry about.

CHAPTER 5

With all the hardships and discomfort that come with STDs, it is important not to lose hope. You are still the same person you always were and deserve the same respect, love, and opportunities that others do. Your experiences dealing with an STD can even bring a sense of personal strength. In time, you can learn to rise above your infection and to approach the future with confidence and pride.

Social Stigma

A major factor in the spread of STDs is the social stigma involved. In other words, those who have gotten an STD are often ashamed of being revealed to their group of friends, or to their entire school. They fear the fallout of losing friends, being the butt of rumors or jokes, or being bullied or treated in even worse ways. In the modern environment of Snapchat, Twitter, Facebook, and other social media, these fears are more justifiable than ever.

These are just a couple of the reasons people who have STDs try to ignore their problem, hoping it just disappears. Although an outbreak might go away, the health risks down the road in leaving STDs untreated are far too dangerous.

You are in control of who knows your most personal secrets, including your health. However,

you cannot always control how others will react to them. Teens with STDs should prepare to deal with the possible fallout they might experience from friends and classmates if their secrets are revealed. Some are unfairly painted with hurtful names and labels. Nobody deserves the horrible misfortune of becoming infected with an STD, but victims sometimes blame themselves. This guilt can make it both harder to tell someone you can trust, and can make you feel worse about yourself, too.

RUMORS AND REALITY

It is not surprising that one of the most common

Although it can often be challenging, facing a problem like an STD infection can help you build the inner strength to move on with your life and even become a better, stronger, and more confident person.

TELLING SOMEONE ELSE'S SECRET

One unenviable situation is getting an STD from a partner, and then realizing that partner is out there engaging in high-risk behavior, even though he or she knows that he or she is infected and could possibly infect others. What do you do then? Do you respect that individual's privacy? Is it that person's decision alone to tell others about the disease?

It is a tough choice, but you must figure out a diplomatic way to help others, despite the shame you might feel in "telling on" someone else. Do not think of it as snitching, or ratting someone out. You might be the only one who can prevent someone else from suffering like you have, and it is your responsibility to take a stand.

rumors that bullies and other classmates make up about a fellow classmate is that they have an STD. This slander arises from the perception that having an STD makes someone disgusting and someone to be avoided. As one anonymous writer contributing to Jenelle Marie's the STD Project website wrote, "If someone has an STD, they're perceived as gross, disgusting, careless, slutty, and judged ferociously." Teens who are not infected (or think they aren't) "believe that if they aren't sleeping with a large number of people, they don't need to be tested. They can sit back and watch it happen to other people while never believing they will come in contact with someone who has an STD."

As statistics show, many more teens who have STDs are unaware that they have them. You are not truly alone in your experience if, say, 20 percent of your high school is going through the same secret ordeal you are. It only takes one sexual experience with a single person to catch an STD. Even if someone has more than one sexual partner and becomes infected, this fact does not make them responsible for getting an STD, or a bad person. Because STDs do not discriminate, it is wrong to judge people. You might overhear a friend talking badly about someone else, claiming that he or she has an STD, or spreading some other rumor. The person doing the talking can just as easily catch one as anyone else.

DEALING WITH DEPRESSION

Many teens who fall into the high-risk groups for getting STDs might suffer depression and other emotional troubles. Going through sadness, anger, or anxiety during the teen years is common. However, those who are diagnosed with an STD, especially if they have symptoms and endure outbreaks, are at particular risk for depression, too. They might blame themselves for their disease, and think they deserved it. Their fear of the shame and embarrassment of revealing this secret might also make things worse.

Another depressing aspect of STD infection is the dramatic effect on one's self-esteem. Many people who have herpes, HPV, and other viral STDs, in particular, hear negative attitudes and commentary about their

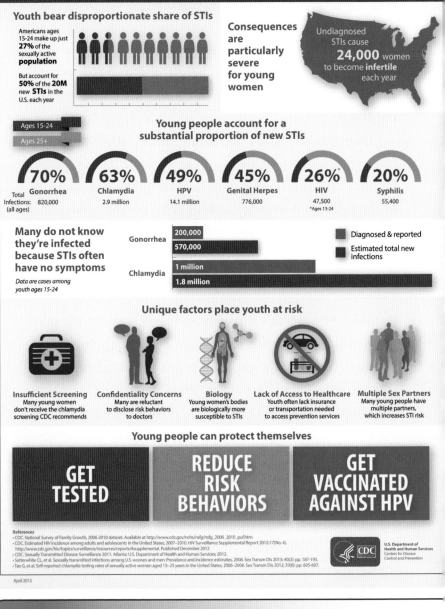

This CDC poster provides a snapshot of the STI/STD infection epidemic that has swept the United States. Education can help remove the stigma and secrecy surrounding the problem.

diseases on a daily basis, usually from friends and others unaware of their infection.

Common negative thoughts can arise: "Nobody will ever want to date me again." "Will I ever get married?" "Will I ever find someone to have children with?" They suffer more from the stigma of the disease than from the disease itself. They might feel repulsive to others and must work extra hard to build back their self-esteem.

Jenelle Marie of the the STD Project told the website Takepart that because STDs are such a taboo subject among teens and adults, that both rarely discuss the emotional impact of STDs. One woman told Marie, "I entered the deepest depression I have ever experienced in the six months following my diagnosis."

If you feel yourself overwhelmed by depression because of your having contracted an STD, it is important to confide in someone, even if you have only revealed this private matter to one or two others so far. Common warning signs are withdrawing from your favorite activities and hobbies, avoiding friends, never leaving your room, or finding that you do not enjoy life like you once did.

Feeling stigmatized, even if no one else knows about your STD, is a feeling that can overwhelm anyone. In extreme cases, people enter severe depression, and some even commit suicide. Many sufferers identify themselves only in terms of the disease, believing it defines them. They can eventually cope by reinforcing

the feeling that although they may have an STD, they are not ruled by it.

Looking on the Bright Side

There might not seem to be a bright side to having an STD, but many people who go through the experience can gain important perspective from it, whether they have bacterial or viral infections, and whether they have symptoms or not. It can make you appreciate good health when you do experience it, and not to take anything for granted.

Another aspect is learning that you cannot judge a book by its cover.

Anxiety, depression, and other emotional problems arising from dealing with STDs can sometimes be crippling. The key is to reach out to others for emotional support.

STDs do not discriminate, and they exist in such a high percentage of the teenage population that you might never know you are talking to someone who might be or might have been affected. The experience of catching an STD also teaches you not to judge others, and that first impressions and initial assumptions about others might be entirely wrong. Consequently, some teens report that the experience builds empathy and compassion. Even if their self-esteem might be affected at first, many teens find that it also makes them stronger people in the long run.

Although STDs can seemingly complicate future relationships, this perception is not always true. Those who are diagnosed might be extra careful in selecting partners in the future. They know the dangers involved in not being selective. They also know that the other person will have to make a decision when the time comes to decide to become intimate or not. They might take the time to build a relationship before engaging in sex, and thus build a stronger foundation. The other person will have to be comfortable with the news of the STD. This revelation

Though it may seem unlikely or even impossible during one's darkest moments, plenty of those who contract STDs go on to have fulfilling and happy relationships.

will filter out those who have less honorable intentions—that is, those who are just looking for sex. The one who sticks around will prove that he or she is worthwhile. More important, that person considers you worthwhile, too.

As mentioned previously, telling other partners (past, present, and future) will also prove to be a character-building exercise. Possessing enough respect for others, and thus telling them about your STD, will have the indirect effect of building your own self-respect and self-esteem. Part of the reason STDs are so common is that many people do not have the strength to be honest with others. When you do make the right decision and take that awkward first step to tell someone, take pride that you yourself had the moral strength of character to do so.

Living Healthy in the Long Term

Teens who have lived through STDs know better than most the necessity of taking care of their health. Even those who have common and curable STDs such as gonorrhea and chlamydia have experienced a rude awakening. Having an STD makes it necessary to keep track of one's health. This care means regular screening, especially if someone remains sexually active. Just because someone has been cured of a bacterial STD, or has been free of viral outbreaks from HPV, for instance, does not mean that he or she is in the clear.

In addition, having an STD also requires that you keep on top of symptom flare-ups. Symptoms of herpes and HPV, for example, might not always be easily apparent. Educate yourself on the warning signs of coming outbreaks. Being prepared will allow you to get ahead of an outbreak with medication, for example.

Being sexually active means always making sure one is protected at all times. Teens experiencing and treating current symptoms, or simply waiting them out, need to avoid sexual activity because their increased contagiousness might endanger others.

Dealing with certain STDs can be more complicated. HIV requires extra commitment. Taking the necessary drugs can prevent future health problems, even as the symptoms of the drugs prescribed to alleviate HIV's risks might be uncomfortable for many patients. Teens with HIV will need more regular doctor visits to track the health of their immune systems, and must make harder choices than others. It is important to remember, however, that many newly infected HIV patients are living longer and more productive lives than previously. Medical science has devised ever more sophisticated and beneficial treatments for HIV as more is learned about the disease.

Thus far, there are no cures for HIV, HPV, herpes, or hepatitis B. However, researchers are making progress on other STDs, such as chronic hepatitis

B. Current treatments slow down the progression of the virus and thus alleviate the liver disease that the infection causes.

A HEALTHY IMMUNE SYSTEM

Viral STDs flare up more for some patients than others. To some extent, one cannot control exactly how one's body reacts over time to these diseases. Most people, including health experts, agree that taking care of your health in general really helps to minimize the long-term effects of STDs. There are many ways to maintain a healthy immune system.

Doctors agree that stress reduction is important for many STD patients' wellbeing. This course of action is especially recommended for herpes sufferers because stress is a major trigger for

In addition to exercise, diet is an important component in boosting a person's immune system. Since STDs can compromise one's health, it is even more vital to maintain proper nutrition.

flare-ups. Immune health for people who have HIV is also incredibly important. Getting enough sleep can reduce stress, too.

A balanced, healthy diet can also aid in preventing STD outbreaks, or alleviating their negative consequences. Eat plenty of fruits and vegetables, and avoid fatty and sugary foods and junk foods. Drink plenty of water. For some people, keeping caffeine intake to a minimum works, as does minimizing or totally eliminating alcohol consumption.

Regular exercise and physical activity are also great for the immune system and stress reduction. They help you feel and look better, too, which contributes to positive self-esteem. Besides moving around, it is important to find ways to relax. These strategies can include activities such as yoga, meditation, or simply quiet activities you enjoy, like reading or doing arts and crafts. Any positive activity that makes you feel good can promote health and give you the extra boost you need to deal with an STD. Taking care of your health will also fuel the positivity you need to avoid depression.

PLAN TO LIVE LIFE TO THE FULLEST

A teen just diagnosed with an STD probably will have many of the anxieties discussed earlier. But life goes on, even with an STD, and that person has the same

Creative pursuits such as painting help STD patients become less tense. At the same time, happiness and stress reduction go hand-in-hand with good health.

chances to do the things in life that everyone has a right to enjoy. These activities include finishing school, going to college and/or working, experiencing adventure, and living his or her dreams. These people can date, fall in love, and start families like everybody else.

Nevertheless, an STD might occasionally disrupt certain plans. Much of the fallout from catching STDs and dealing with them also comes from the emotional reactions to the condition and its social stigma. If you have the right outlook, plan properly, and take advantage of the support of friends, family, and medical professionals, you can make sure that you control your life and that it is not controlled by your STD.

GLOSSARY

acute Sudden, brief, and severe, as in an acute illness.

antibiotics Powerful medicines used to fight bacterial infections.

antiviral Refers to medicines that stop or slow disease-causing viruses from multiplying in the body.

bacteria Microscopic organisms that can spread and cause human diseases, such as STDs.

CD4+ cell Also known as a CD4+ T-helper cell, a type of white blood cell that is particularly valuable in fighting HIV infection.

cervix The narrow neck-like passage forming the lower end of the uterus in a woman's reproductive system.

chronic Refers to symptoms or a disorder that have lingered for a long period of time.

cryotherapy A treatment for HPV in which abnormal cells are removed by freezing them.

discharge Unusual fluid that comes out of the vagina or penis due to an STD infection.

infertility The inability to produce offspring.

latent Used to describe a disease that exists but is not active or has not produced any noticeable symptoms.

monogamy Only having one sexual partner at a time.

outbreak A time when STD symptoms occur.

promiscuity The state of being promiscuous, or having many sexual partners.

protozoa Single-celled organisms that live in moist or wet environments, including the human body.

screening Testing for the presence of a condition or disease such as an STD.

serial monogamy Practicing monogamy, but changing partners frequently.

social stigma The social shame that someone experiences because they are different or because they have done something wrong or considered wrong by others.

STD Short for sexually transmitted disease, an infection spread through sexual contact.

STI Short for sexually transmitted infection, another name for STDs.

swab A cotton ball on a stick used to take biological samples for testing.

virus A microscopic, infectious agent that needs another organism's living cells to make copies of itself, often causing disease in the process.

FOR MORE INFORMATION

AIDS Action Committee (AAC)
75 Armory Street
Roxbury, MA 02119
(800) 235-2231
Website: http://www.aac.org

The AIDS Action Committee provides resources to help those suffering from STDs, including its anonymous STD411 hotline.

Advocates for Youth
2000 M Street NW, Suite 750
Washington, DC 20036
(202) 419-3420
Website: http://www.advocatesforyouth.org

Advocates for Youth promotes support for adolescent sexual health initiatives, including STD education, prevention, screening, and treatment.

American Sexual Health Association (ASHA)
P.O. Box 13827
Research Triangle Park, NC 27709
(800) 227-8922; STD hotline: (919) 361-8488
Website: http://www.ashastd.org

This organization gives out educational materials about STD infections and provides confidential information on STDs and referrals to clinical services.

American Sexually Transmitted Diseases Association (ASTDA)

P.O. Box 12665
Research Triangle Park, NC 27709
(919) 861-9399
Website: http://www.astda.org

The ASTDA is an organization of groups and individuals, with membership open to anyone involved in the control and prevention of STDs.

Centers for Disease Control and Prevention (CDC)

1600 Clifton Road
Atlanta, GA 30333
CDC National STD Hotline: (800) 232-4636
Website: http://www.cdc.gov

The CDC is the federal agency dedicated to promoting public health and safety by preventing the spread of diseases, and preventing injury and disability.

Foundation for Research on Sexually Transmitted Diseases (FROSTD.org)

290 Lenox Avenue, Lower Level
New York, NY 10027
(212) 924-3733
Website: http://www.frostd.org

FROSTD.org is a nonprofit, community-based organization that offers help to medically underserved communities and sufferers of AIDS and other STDs.

Gay Men's Health Crisis (GMHC)

446 West 33rd Street

New York, NY 10001-2601
(212) 367-1000
Website: http://www.gmhc.org

GMHC was the first advocacy group to push for recognition of HIV/ AIDS victims, and fights to end HIV/AIDS infection worldwide.

Health Canada
Address Locator 0900C2
Ottawa, ON K1A 0K9
Canada
(613) 957-2991
Website: http://www.hc-sc.gc.ca

Health Canada is the leading national public health governmental agency in Canada, with part of its mandate the tracking and prevention of sexually transmitted infections.

Planned Parenthood Federation of America
434 West 33rd Street
New York, NY 10001
(212) 541-7800;
Sexual health hotline: (800) 230-PLAN (7526)
Website: http://www.plannedparenthood.org

Planned Parenthood is a leading provider of reproductive health care with numerous offices nationwide. It also provides STD testing and counseling.

**Sex Information and Education Council of
    Canada (SIECCAN)**
850 Coxwell Avenue
Toronto, ON M4C 5R1

Canada

(416) 466-5304

Website: http://www.sieccan.org

SIECCAN is a Canadian charitable organization that fosters professional education and public knowledge about sexuality and sexual health, including educational efforts in public schools.

WEBSITE

Because of the changing nature of Internet links, Rosen Publishing has developed an online list of websites related to the subject of this book. This site is updated regularly. Please use this link to access the list:

http://www.rosenlinks.com/411/STD

FOR FURTHER READING

Ambrose, Marylou, and Veronica Deisler. *Investigating STDs (Sexually Transmitted Diseases): Real Facts for Real Lives* (Investigating Diseases). Berkeley Heights, NJ: Enslow Publishers, 2010.

Berlatsky, Noah. *HIV/AIDS* (Global Viewpoints). Farmington Hills, MI: Greenhaven Press, 2011.

Breguet, Amy. *Chlamydia* (Library of Sexual Health). New York, NY: Rosen Publishing Group, 2006.

Bringle, Jennifer. *Reproductive Rights: Making the Right Choices* (A Young Woman's Guide to Contemporary Issues). New York, NY: Rosen Publishing Group, 2010.

Bringle, Jennifer. *Young Women and the HPV Vaccine*. New York, NY: Rosen Publishing, 2012.

Collins, Nicholas, and Samuel G. Woods. *Frequently Asked Questions About STDs* (FAQ: Teen Life). New York, NY: Rosen Publishing Group, 2011.

Connolly, Sean. *STDs* (Just the Facts). Portsmouth, NH: Heinemann Library, 2002.

Cozic, Charles P. *Herpes* (Compact Research: Diseases & Disorders). San Diego, CA: ReferencePoint Press, 2011.

Currie-McGhee, Leanne K. *Sexually Transmitted Diseases* (Compact Research). San Diego, CA: ReferencePoint Press, 2008.

Dittmer, Lori. *HIV/AIDS* (Living with Disease). Mankato, MN: Creative Education, 2011.

Dougherty, Terri. *Sexually Transmitted Diseases* (Diseases & Disorders). Farmington Hills, MI: Lucent Books, 2010.

Espejo, Roman. *Sexually Transmitted Diseases* (Opposing Viewpoints). Farmington Hills, MI: Greenhaven Press, 2011.

Ford, Carol A., and Elizabeth Shimer Bowers. *Living with Sexually Transmitted Diseases* (Teen's Guides). New York, NY: Facts On File, 2009.

Langwith, Jacqueline, ed. *HPV* (Perspectives on Diseases and Disorders). Farmington Hills, MI: Greenhaven Press, 2013.

Michaud, Christopher. *Gonorrhea* (The Library of Sexual Health). New York, NY: Rosen Publishing, 2007.

Naff, Clayton Farris. *Sexually Transmitted Diseases* (Perspectives on Diseases & Disorders). Farmington Hills, MI: Greenhaven Press, 2008.

Ozer, Yvette Malamud, ed. *A Student Guide to Health: Understanding the Facts, Trends, and Challenges.* 5 volumes. Santa Barbara, CA: ABC-CLIO, 2012.

Parks, Peggy J. *Sexually Transmitted Diseases* (Compact Research). San Diego, CA: ReferencePoint Press, 2013.

Robinson, Richard. *Frequently Asked Questions About AIDS and HIV* (Teen Life FAQ). New York, NY: Rosen Publishing, 2009.

Shmaefsky, Brian R. *Gonorrhea* (Deadly Diseases and Epidemics). New York, NY: Chelsea House Publishers, 2010.

Shmaefsky, Brian. *Syphilis* (Deadly Diseases and Epidemics). New York, NY: Chelsea House Publishers, 2009.

Vincent, Beverly, and Robert Greenberger. *Frequently Asked Questions About Birth Control* (FAQ: Teen Life). New York, NY: Rosen Publishing Group, 2011.

Yancey, Diane. *STDs* (*USA Today* Health Reports: Diseases & Disorders). Minneapolis, MN: Twenty-First Century Books, 2011.

BIBLIOGRAPHY

Alexander, Brian. "'Ongoing, Severe' Epidemic of STDs in US, Report Finds." *NBC News*, February 13, 2013. Retrieved February 2, 2014 (http://vitals.nbcnews.com/_news/2013/02/13/16951432-ongoing-severe-epidemic-of-stds-in-us-report-finds).

Benfield, Priscilla. "How to Deal with Having an STD." Yahoo! Voices, November 30, 2010. Retrieved February 7, 2014 (http://voices.yahoo.com/how-deal-having-std-7306702.html).

Burns, Nick. "The Risks: HIV, Herpes, HPV (Warts), Syphilis, Chlamydia, Gonorrhea, Hepatitis B." Health, May 11, 2008. Retrieved February 2, 2014 (http://www.health.com/health/condition-article/0,,20188708,00.html).

Carnegie Mellon University. "Teens Unaware of Sexually Transmitted Diseases Until They Catch One, Carnegie Mellon Study Finds." ScienceDaily, January 4, 2006. Retrieved January 21, 2014 (http://www.sciencedaily.com/releases/2006/01/060103182708.htm).

Centers for Disease Control and Prevention. "Sexually Transmitted Diseases (STDs)."Retrieved January 4, 2014 (http://www.cdc.gov/std/default.htm).

Doherty, Shawn. "Rates of STDs Among Teens Reach Epidemic Levels." *Capital Times*, January 6,

2010. Retrieved January 20, 2014 (http://
host.madison.com/news/local/health_med_fit/
rates-of-stds-among-teens-reach-epidemic-levels/
article_96d0ee57-e3dc-59d7-a5ec-e5cbc5b7
1ffc.html).

Dunn, Gaby. "The Strongest Herpes Support Group
Is on Tumblr." The Daily Dot, June 28, 2013.
Retrieved January 29, 2014 (http://www.dailydot
.com/lifestyle/herpblr-tumblr-herpes-hsv-glitter).

Fitzgerald, Kelly. "STDs Are an Epidemic in the U.S.,
CDC Warns." Medical News Today, February 15,
2013. Retrieved January 19, 2014 (http://www
.medicalnewstoday.com/articles/256413.php).

Gulati, Richa. "What You Need to Know About
STDs." Teen Vogue, November 2012. Retrieved
January 28, 2014 (http://www.teenvogue.com/
beauty/health-fitness/2012-11/what-is-an-std
-hpv-chlamydia).

Holmes, King K., P. Frederick Sparling, Walter
E. Stamm, Peter Piot, Judith N. Wasserheit,
Lawrence Corey, Myron S. Cohen, and D.
Heather Watts. Sexually Transmitted Diseases.
New York, NY: McGraw-Hill, 2007.

Marie, Janelle. "Is 'Slut-Shaming' Contributing to
the Rise of STDs?" TakePart.com, April 29, 2013.
Retrieved December 29, 2013 (http://www
.takepart.com/article/2013/04/29/one-great-way
-stop-stds-stop-calling-people-sluts-skanks-and
-whores).

Marie, Jenelle. "Should I Tell Past Partners I Have a Sexually Transmitted Infection?" The STD Project. Retrieved January 12, 2014 (http://www.thestdproject.com/should-i-tell-past-partners-i-have-a-sexually-transmitted-infection).

Marie, Jenelle. "You Know What's Depressing? Finding Out You Have an STD." TakePart.com, April 26, 2013. Retrieved December 20, 2013 (http://www.takepart.com/article/2013/04/26/stds-mental-health-and-depression).

McDonough, Katie. "Michael Douglas: HPV Caused My Throat Cancer." Salon, June 2, 2013. Retrieved December 29, 2013 (http://www.salon.com/2013/06/02/michael_douglas_hpv_caused_my_throat_cancer).

National Center on Addiction and Substance Abuse at Columbia University. "National Survey on American Attitudes on Substance Abuse XVII: Teens." August 2012. Survey Conducted by QEV Analytics, Ltd. Retrieved March 14, 2014 (http://www.casacolumbia.org/addiction-research/reports/national-survey-american-attitudes-substance-abuse-teens-2012).

Planned Parenthood. "Half of All Teens Feel Uncomfortable Talking to Their Parents About Sex While Only 19 Percent of Parents Feel the Same, New Survey Shows." Press release, October 2, 2012. Retrieved January 20, 2014 (http://www.plannedparenthood.org/about-us/newsroom/

press-releases/half-all-teens-feel-uncomfortable
-talking-their-parents-about-sex-while-only-19
-percent-parents-40375.htm).

Planned Parenthood. "Safer Sex ('Safe Sex')." 2014.
Retrieved January 2, 2014 (http://www
.plannedparenthood.org/health-topics/stds
-hiv-safer-sex-101.htm).

Ross, Linda M. (ed). *Sexually Transmitted Diseases
Sourcebook*. Detroit, MI: Omnigraphics, 2009.

Spiesel, Sydney. "The State of the STD: The CDC's
Updated Stats on Sexually Transmitted Diseases."
Slate, January 16, 2009. Retrieved January 22, 2014
(http://www.slate.com/articles/health_and_science/
whats_up_doc/2009/01/the_state_of_the_std.html).

USA Today. "1 in 4 Teen Girls Have STD." May
27, 2008. Retrieved December 14, 2013 (http://
usatoday30.usatoday.com/news/health/2008-03-
11-std_n.htm).

INDEX

ABOUT THE AUTHOR

Philip Wolny is a writer and editor from Queens, New York. His other health-related titles for Rosen Publishing aimed at young people include *Incredibly Disgusting Drugs: Abusing Prescription Drugs* and *The Truth About Heroin.*

PHOTO CREDITS

Cover, p. 1 Dmitry Kalinovsky/iStock/Thinkstock; p. 5 Lemoine/BSIP/SuperStock; pp. 8–9 Seth Joel/Photographer's Choice/Getty Images; pp. 12–13 Len44ik/Shutterstock.com; pp. 15 (top), 50 Alila Medical Media/Shutterstock.com; p. 15 (bottom) BlueRingMedia/Shutterstock.com; pp. 18–19 Joe Schilling/Time & Life Pictures/Getty Images; pp. 20–21, 62–63 Alexander Raths/Shutterstock.com; p. 26–27, 54–55 BSIP/Universal Images Group/Getty Images; pp. 30–31 Stocktrek Image/Getty Images; pp. 34–35, 36–37 Biophoto Associates/Photo Researchers/Getty Images; pp. 38–39 Dr. P. Marazzi/Science Source; pp. 42–43 Science Picture Co/Collection Mix: Subjects/Getty Images; p. 47 Michelle Del Guercio/Photo Researchers/Getty Images; pp. 52–53 Science Source; p. 58 Bo Veisland/Science Source; p. 60 Dr. Martin Baumgärtne/imagebroker.net/SuperStock; pp. 66–67 Mark Herreid/Shutterstock.com; pp. 70–71 Huy Lam/First Light/Getty Images; p. 73 Jupiterimages/Pixland/Thinkstock; pp. 74–75 jeebbus/iStock/Thinkstock; pp. 78–79 szefei/Shutterstock.com; p. 82 CDC – NCHHSTP; pp. 84–85 Antonio Guillem/Shutterstock.com; pp. 86-87 DreamPictures/Photodisc/Getty Images; pp. 90–91Lucky Business/Shutterstock.com; p. 93 George Dolgikh/Shutterstock.com.

Designer: Les Kanturek; Editor: Kathy Kuhtz Campbell; Photo Researcher: Marty Levick